THE POCKET

Beyoncé

Published in 2025
by Gemini Books
Part of Gemini Books Group

Based in Woodbridge and London

Marine House, Tide Mill Way,
Woodbridge, Suffolk IP12 1AP
United Kingdom
www.geminibooks.com

Text and Design © 2025 Gemini Adult Books Ltd
Part of the Gemini Pockets series

Cover illustration by Natalie Floss

ISBN 978-1-80247-277-6

A CIP catalogue record for this book is available from the British Library.

Disclaimer: The book is a guidebook purely for information and
entertainment purposes only. All trademarks, individual and company
names, brand names, registered names, quotations, celebrity names,
logos, dialogues and catchphrases used or cited in this book are the
property of their respective owners. The publisher does not assume
and hereby disclaims any liability to any party for any loss, damage
or disruption caused by errors or omissions, whether such errors or
omissions result from negligence, accident or any other cause. This book
is an unofficial and unauthorized publication by Gemini Adult Books
Ltd and has not been licensed, approved, sponsored or endorsed by
Beyoncé or any other person or entity.

Printed in China

10 9 8 7 6 5 4 3 2 1

Images: Alamy: 4, 7, 64, 96 / Associated Press; 8 / Sipa US; 36 / Rob Watkins.
Shutterstock: 28, 43 / Tassia_K. Freepik: 19, 22, 60, 63, 80, 111, 119.

THE
POCKET

Beyoncé

G:

CONTENTS

Introduction

Beyoncé's influence as the world's greatest living entertainer shows no signs of abating, even as she approaches her 25th year in the spotlight.

From a '90s child of destiny, through the peak of her star's zenith – around 2013, when she dominated pop culture – and beyond, Beyoncé is an alchemist: everything she touches turns to platinum and gold.

Today, Queen Bey is as relevant, and as essential, as she's ever been. An acclaimed musician, filmmaker, actor and empire-builder, as well as a married mother of three, Beyoncé quite simply runs the world. Long may she reign!

Chapter One

Dream Girl

4 September 1981

Baby Bey is born! Her parents, Mathew and Tina Knowles, have been with Beyoncé for every step of her success, with her father even quitting his job as a printer salesman to manage his daughter's fledgling girl-group, Destiny's Child.

It was while being raised as a Methodist in Houston, Texas, that Beyoncé was first encouraged to sing in the gospel choir – at St John's United Methodist Church. There, she refined her vocal abilities and learnt the skill and discipline it takes to sing as part of a harmonic group. Beyoncé reflects on these soulful beginnings on the 2022 track 'Church Girl', from the album *Renaissance*.

Beyoncé is the eighth most followed
celebrity *in the world* on Instagram
with 316 million followers.

The other Top 10 Insta big-hitters
currently include: Cristiano Ronaldo,
Lionel Messi, Selena Gomez, Kim and
Khloe Kardashian, Justin Bieber, Kylie
Jenner, Dwayne (The Rock) Johnson
and Ariana Grande.

In 2003, while still a member of Destiny's Child, Beyoncé released her solo album, *Dangerously In Love*. It was a critical and commercial hit selling more than 11 million copies. Its stand-out track was, of course, 'Crazy In Love', a collaboration with her boyfriend Jay-Z. This success proved that anything Destiny's Child could do, Beyoncé could do better.

The record won five Grammys in 2004, including Best Contemporary R'n'B Album, giving Beyoncé the opportunity to sing 'Dangerously In Love 2' on stage at the ceremony alongside her hero, Prince.

Essential Album
#1: *Dangerously In Love*

1. 'Crazy In Love' (ft. Jay-Z)

2. 'Naughty Girl'

3. 'Baby Boy' (ft. Sean Paul)

4. 'Hip Hop Star' (ft. Big Boi & Sleepy Brown)

5. 'Be With You'

6. 'Me, Myself and I'

7. 'Yes'

8. 'Signs' (ft. Missy Elliott)

9. 'Speechless'

10. 'That's How You Like It' (ft. Jay-Z)

11. 'The Closer I Get to You' with Luther Vandross (ft. Beyoncé)

12. 'Dangerously In Love'

13. 'Gift from Virgo'

14. 'Daddy'

"I'm more powerful than my mind can even digest and understand."

Beyoncé, GQ, January 2013

Single Covers

Beyoncé has more than 55 million monthly listens on Spotify, making her songs some of the most played on the planet.

With a catalogue of more than 200 songs to choose from, these are the most-streamed:

1. 'Halo' – *1.6 billion streams*!
2. 'Crazy In Love'
3. 'Cuff It'
4. 'Single Ladies (Put a Ring on It)'
5. 'Love On Top'
6. 'Irreplaceable'
7. 'Texas Hold 'Em'
8. 'If I Were a Boy'
9. 'Baby Boy'
10. 'Beautiful Liar'

Search for a Star

In 1990, when Beyoncé was just nine years old, she joined a six-person, all-girl singing group called Girl's Tyme with friend Kelly Rowland. The group was put together by a local producer who was impressed by their raw talent.

The group's first big performance was on *Star Search* – America's iconic TV variety show, watched by tens of millions each week – where they sang 'Flawless', written by Beyoncé. Winners of the show won $100,000, but sadly Girl's Tyme lost out to Skeleton Crew.* The girls received a score of 3.5 stars out of four from the judges. Beyoncé would later use an excerpt from the performance on her 2013 album, *Beyoncé.*

*Never to be heard of again.

"It was wonderful to be a kid and be on television. When we lost, we just balled our eyes out. But our parents took us to Disney World so it was all good, like nothing ever happened. But we were kids, we thought we were gonna win!"

Beyoncé, *The Tonight Show with Jay Leno*, 2007

Beyhive

The term used to refer to the fandom of Beyoncé.*

*Presumably if you're reading this
you belong to the hive?

The Beyhive

In an interview in *Vogue* (November 2020), Beyoncé revealed herself to be a proud owner of two beehives. She claimed she keeps more than 80,000 bees – enough to make "hundreds of jars of honey" a year.

"I know it's random," she said, "but I started the beehives because my daughters, Blue and Rumi, both have terrible allergies, and honey has countless healing properties."

Keeping Bey Alive

Beyoncé's famous mononym comes from her mother's maiden surname before she married Mathew Knowles. Tina Knowles-Lawson's birth name was Celestine Beyoncé.

"Beyoncé is my last name, my maiden name. When I was gonna have a baby, we have very few boys, and so I was like, 'Oh, God, this name is gonna become extinct.'"

Tina Knowles-Lawson, *Vogue*, May 2024

*

Beyoncé
is pronounced
bih-yown-sey,

not
bey-yown-sey,
by the way.

Imagine...

When Beyoncé was just seven years old her father Mathew entered her into her first school talent show after being told by dance teacher, Darlette Johnson, that his daughter had the "X Factor". There, she competed against singers twice her age. She sang John Lennon's 'Imagine'. And won!

After smashing her first talent show, little Bey went on to win the next *35 talent shows in a row!*

" Sometimes I think that after a while I'm going to move away and sing in a bar somewhere, because I am a little afraid of being too famous. "

Beyoncé, *The Daily Telegraph*, July 2002

Woman of Every Year

In 2009, Beyoncé received Billboard's
prestigious Woman of the Year Award.
The trophy celebrated and acknowledged
Beyoncé's dominance as a cultural force
following the global success of her third
album and its many hit singles.

If you're wondering which album sent
Beyoncé supersonic, look no further than
I Am... Sasha Fierce.

Dictionary-defining Moments

The term "Bootylicious" first appeared on record in the 1992 song 'Dre Day' by Snoop Dogg, but it was the 2001 hit track by Destiny's Child that led to an explosion in the use of the word, cementing its place in the lexicon of popular culture.

For those that can remember, bootylicious-ness was everywhere in the early noughties. It was so widespread, in fact, that the word was added to the *Oxford English Dictionary* in 2004.

Bootylicious

(adj.)

(of a woman)
sexually attractive.

Beyoncé

Essential Album #2:
I Am... Sasha Fierce

1. 'If I Were a Boy'
2. 'Halo'
3. 'Disappear'
4. 'Broken-hearted Girl'
5. 'Ave Maria'
6. 'Satellites'
7. 'Single Ladies (Put a Ring on It)'
8. 'Radio'
9. 'Diva'
10. 'Sweet Dreams'
11. 'Video Phone' (ft. Lady Gaga)

Meet Sasha

For the release of her 2008 album, *I Am... Sasha Fierce*, Beyoncé brought her alter-ego out to play. Ms Fierce allowed the singer to express more dynamic, bold and fearless elements of her personality on stage.

The album sold 10 million copies – it's easily her biggest-selling album – and contained iconic hits 'Single Ladies (Put a Ring on It)' and 'Halo'. It also earned her six Grammy Awards, breaking the record for most awards ever won by a female artist in one night.

Grammy G.O.A.T.

With Destiny's Child, Beyoncé collected her first ever Grammy Award in 2001, aged just 20, for the worldwide hit, 'Say My Name'.

Two decades later, at the 65th Annual Grammy Awards in 2023, the singer-songwriter made history when she became the *most honoured artist of all time* winning a total of 32 awards (from 88 nominations)*, when she won Best Dance/Electronic Recording for 'Break My Soul' from the album *Renaissance*.

*Spookily, Jay-Z shares the same number of Grammy nominations.

"I'd like to thank my parents, my father, my mother, for loving me and pushing me. I'd like to thank my beautiful husband, my beautiful three children, who are at home watching. I'd like to thank the queer community for your love and for inventing this genre. God bless you."

Beyoncé, from her speech at the 65th Annual Grammy Awards, 5 February 2023

» We decide everything together. My word is my word. What Jay and I have is real. It's not about interviews or getting the right photo op. It's real. »

Beyoncé, *Essence*, 16 December 2009

The Carters

Beyoncé and rapper Jay-Z tied the knot on 4 April 2008. The service was held at Jay-Z's New York penthouse under a large white canopy in his living room!

They first met in 1999 and began dating when Beyoncé was 19. They have been through tough times – but the Carters remain strong today.

On-screen Queen

Beyoncé has starred in several big-screen blockbusters and cult classics, each showing her versatility and emotional depth as an actor. How many of these have you seen?

1. *Carmen: A Hip Hopera* (2001)

2. *Austin Powers in Goldmember* (2002)

3. *The Fighting Temptations* (2003)

4. *Fade to Black* (2004)

5. *The Pink Panther* (2006)

6. *Dreamgirls* (2006)

7. *Cadillac Records* (2008)

8. *Obsessed* (2009)

9. *Epic* (voice, 2013)

10. *The Lion King* (voice, 2019)

11. *Mufasa: The Lion King* (voice, 2024)

" I took a risk with acting.
It was scary because it
was different for me.
You just always have to
take risks. I always go
with my gut, and it's
always right. People
are scared to do that. "

Beyoncé, *Cosmopolitan*, November 2006

Chapter Two
A Child of Destiny

Beyoncé

Before Beyoncé became a single lady, Destiny's Child racked up a wealth of hits, awards and streams. Today, the group still earn 15 million Spotify listens a month! Here is a list of their biggest hits:

1. 'Say My Name' – *900 million streams!*

2. 'Survivor'

3. 'Jumpin', Jumpin''

4. 'Bills, Bills, Bills'

5. 'Independent Women Part I'

6. 'Lose My Breath'

7. 'Bootylicious'

8. 'Cater 2 U'

9. 'Brown Eyes'

10. 'Soldier'

"There would definitely not be a Beyoncé without Destiny's Child. I love my girls."

Beyoncé, ABC News, November 2009

6801 Hollywood Boulevard

This is the address of Destiny's Child's star on the Hollywood Walk of Fame.

The group received its star in 2006, following the band's break-up. Beyoncé is yet to receive the same accolade for her solo work, but there's still plenty of time.

Destiny Awaits

In 1995, Mathew Knowles began managing his daughter's group. At first – around 1990 – the group were called Girl's Tyme, then Somethin' Fresh, followed by Cliché, and then the Dolls. They finally settled on Destiny, a word suggested by Beyoncé's mother, Tina. Mathew's first order of business was to reduce the number of girls to four, leaving Beyoncé, Kelly Rowland, LaTavia Roberson and LeToya Luckett.

In 1996, the group set their name to Destiny's Child, taking inspiration from a passage from the Bible, Isaiah 65:11–12.

Debut R'n'B album, *Destiny's Child* (1998), wasn't an overnight sensation. However, its follow-up, the neo-soul-stuffed classic *The Writing's on the Wall* (1999), was. It set Beyoncé on her path to greatness and has sold more than 13 million copies.

Essential Album
#3: *The Writing's on the Wall*

1. 'Intro (The Writing's on the Wall)'
2. 'So Good'
3. 'Bills, Bills, Bills'
4. 'Confessions' (ft. Missy Elliott)
5. 'Bug a Boo'
6. 'Temptation'
7. 'Now That She's Gone'
8. 'Where'd You Go'
9. 'Hey Ladies'
10. 'If You Leave' (ft. Next)
11. 'Jumpin', Jumpin'
12. 'Say My Name'
13. 'She Can't Love You'
14. 'Stay'
15. 'Sweet Sixteen'
16. 'Outro (Amazing Grace... dedicated to Andretta Tillman)'

First – but Certainly Not Last

It was 2001's *Survivor* album that made Beyoncé and her bandmates a household name. This 15-track masterpiece became Beyoncé's first No. 1 record and has since gone on to sell more than 10 million copies worldwide! It features the R'n'B bangers 'Independent Women Part I', 'Survivor', 'Bootylicious' and 'Dangerously In Love'.

It also marks the moment when two of the group's founding members – LeToya Luckett and LaTavia Roberson – left the group, replaced by Michelle Williams to fill out the famous trio (with Beyoncé and Kelly Rowland).

" *Survivor*'s a testimony
to how close we've
become as a group.
We managed to have a
great time working on
this album as a team. "

Beyoncé, *Billboard*, May 2001

'Independent Women
Part I' stayed at No. 1 for
11 consecutive weeks
– earning the group a
Guinness World Record for
the longest-running No. 1
song by a female group.

A Trio of Angels

In August 2000, Destiny's Child released what was to become their signature song – 'Independent Women Part I'.

The track became the official theme of the *Charlie's Angels* movie, which featured three more independent women: Drew Barrymore, Cameron Diaz and Lucy Liu. Beyoncé's father, Mathew, actually submitted the track for consideration without telling the group and when Beyoncé found out she rewrote the lyrics to fit the film.

Crazy in Love

The world went crazy in love for Beyoncé's debut solo single (featuring Jay-Z), released more than 20 years ago – in May 2003. It is considered her signature song, and is regularly voted one of the greatest pop songs of all time.

The tune sold 6 million copies and stayed at No. 1 on the Billboard chart for eight consecutive weeks. It was also the song that Beyoncé and Jay-Z first danced to when they got married!

\\ 'Crazy In Love' was another one of those classic moments in pop culture that none of us expected. It still never gets old, no matter how many times I sing it. \\

Beyoncé, *Billboard*, November 2011

" I started my own company when I decided to manage myself. I wanted to follow the footsteps of Madonna and have my own empire, and show other women when you get to this point in your career you don't have to go sign with someone else and share your money and your success – you do it yourself. "

Beyoncé, *Billboard*, 2014

Innovative All Round

In 2008, Beyoncé founded her own multimedia
company, Parkwood Entertainment, as a means
to distribute a variety of projects she was
working on.

To date, Beyoncé has used Parkwood to fund
the musical biopic *Cadillac Records* (2008) that
she starred in, and the visual albums *Lemonade*
and *Homecoming*.

In 2017 the company was voted one of the USA's
10 Most Innovative Companies in Music.

Collaborative Couple

Beyoncé and her husband Jay-Z have shared much more than wedding vows. The singer and rapper have also collaborated creatively several times (excluding their three children).

The pair first worked together on Jay-Z's '03 Bonnie and Clyde' (2002), as well as 2003's 'Crazy In Love', 2006's 'Déjà Vu', 2013's 'Drunk In Love', 2014's On the Run Tour, and 2018's *Everything Is Love*, an album the couple released under the name The Carters.

In total, the couple have collabed on more than 50 songs together to date.

In 2014, Beyoncé won the Lifetime Achievement Award at the 2014 MTV VMAs. She was just 32 years old.

The award was presented to Beyoncé by Jay-Z and her two-year-old daughter Blue Ivy (who screamed "Mommy!" down the microphone).

"I'm somebody,
and nobody's
gonna hold
me down...
I'm somebody!"

Deena Jones (Beyoncé), *Dreamgirls*, 2006

Dream Girl

While Beyoncé has appeared in more than ten feature-length movies, it is with *Dreamgirls* in 2006 that she first received critical acclaim.

Taking its inspiration from the life and times of the Supremes – the R'n'B supergroup that rose to fame in the 1960s and 1970s with Diana Ross as its leader – *Dreamgirls* is a musical biopic that sees Beyoncé play Deena Jones (a character inspired by Ross) reaching for the stars.

The film was a box office success, and received eight Academy Award nominations. Jennifer Hudson won Best Supporting Actress and Beyoncé earned a Golden Globe nomination for Best Actress.

Gladiators

On 26 January 2004, pop culture changed forever when three of its biggest stars – Britney Spears, Beyoncé and P!nk – united for the then-most expensive advert of all time – Pepsi's Super Bowl halftime show "Gladiator" advert – said to have cost $2 million (£1.5 million).

The trio were flown to Rome to film at the Colosseum. There, they transformed into gladiators ready to do battle and defy the Emperor (Enrique Iglesias) by singing Queen's 'We Will Rock You', after drinking his stash of ice-cold Pepsi.

If it sounds ridiculous that's because it is. More than 90 million people watched the advert on the day of the Super Bowl. On YouTube, the advert now has more than 40 million views.

"Beyoncé is the prettiest person you could ever stand in front of. She glows like a goddess!"

P!nk, *People*, 2022

"I'm really happy for you, but Beyoncé had one of the best videos of all time. *Of all time.*"

Kanye West, to Taylor Swift, MTV VMAs, 2009

"Oh My God"

At the infamous 2009 MTV Video Music Awards Taylor Swift won Best Female Video, only to have her acceptance speech invaded by the rapper Kanye West, who proclaimed Beyoncé should have won instead. The camera cuts to Beyoncé mouthing, "Oh my God." Everyone is in shock. (*Rolling Stone* voted it the year's wildest moment.)

Later in the ceremony, Beyoncé won Video of the Year for 'Single Ladies (Put a Ring on It)' and invited Taylor Swift onto the stage to finish her speech. Pure class.

Grammy Goddess

Beyoncé made history at the 52nd annual Grammy Awards in January 2010 when she won a record number of awards for a female artist – six Grammy wins in a single night!

Her trophies were for the sought-after Song of the Year ('Single Ladies (Put a Ring on It)'), Best Female Pop Vocal Performance ('Halo'), Best Female R'n'B Vocal Performance, Best Traditional R'n'B Vocal Performance, Best R'n'B Song and Best Contemporary R'n'B Album (*I Am... Sasha Fierce*).

"I'm not bossy.
I'm the boss."

Beyoncé, *Rolling Stone*, 10 March 2014

Essential Album #4: *Lemonade*

Taking its name from the proverbial phrase, "If life gives you lemons, make lemonade", 2016's (visual) album, *Lemonade* is said to be inspired by husband Jay-Z's infidelities.

The album is divided into 11 chapters, each one a stage of Beyoncé's emotional state while dealing with the aftermath: Intuition, Denial, Anger, Apathy, Emptiness, Accountability, Reformation, Forgiveness, Resurrection, Hope and Redemption.

Upon its release it was critically acclaimed and has since become rated as one of the greatest albums of all time, winning two Grammys and a (highly prestigious) Peabody Award for its visual album directed by, of course, Beyoncé, with others.

Beyonce's recipe for lemonade
(as heard in *Homecoming*, 2013)
goes something like this:

"One pint of water, add a half-pound
of sugar, the juice of eight lemons, and
the zest of half of a lemon.
Pour the water from one jug into the
other several times, strain through a
clean napkin."

Chapter Three
Happy B-day

Only two solo artists in the history of pop music have enjoyed No. 1 Billboard hits in four different decades: the 1990s, the 2000s, the 2010s and the 2020s. Beyoncé is one. Can you guess the other?

Answer below.

Mariah Carey

"I'm never satisfied. I've never met anyone that works harder than me in my industry. I'm sure sometimes it's not easy working for me."

Beyoncé, *Forbes*, June 2009

" I don't need Sasha
Fierce so much anymore
because these days I know
who I am. Sasha Fierce
is done. I killed her. "

Beyoncé, *Allure*, January 2010

Goodbye, Sasha & Mathew

In 2010, Beyoncé not only killed off her alter-ego Sasha Fierce, she also parted ways with her father Mathew Knowles as her manager.

Mathew went on to focus on the genres of country, gospel and children's under his Music World label, which he eventually sold in 2022.

Super Bey

Beyoncé has performed at the Super Bowl halftime extravaganza more than any other modern performer. And for good reason: her first performance in 2013 catapulted her to become a cultural icon. The show also reunited her with her Destiny's Child bandmates – and amassed 110.8 million viewers. The 12-minute setlist was incredible:

'Run the World (Girls)', 'Love On Top', 'Crazy In Love', 'End of Time', 'Baby Boy', 'Bootylicious', 'Independent Women Part I', 'Single Ladies (Put a Ring on It)' and 'Halo'.

"I approach my shows like an athlete. It's one of the reasons I connect to the Super Bowl."

Beyoncé, GQ, January 2013

Feel the Burn

Beyoncé is one supremely fit human. She is famed for her energy and stamina during her live performances, as well as being able to sing and dance – in heels! – flawlessly at the same time. During her routines, she burns more than 1,500 calories for every two-hour performance.

World's Most Beautiful

Beyoncé has won countless awards for her music in her 25-year career. She has also won many for her looks, most notably in 2012 when she was named the "World's Most Beautiful Woman" by *People* magazine.

This award was of particular significance as it came just three months after Beyoncé gave birth to her daughter, Blue Ivy, in January 2012, and was the first time a new mother had been awarded the title.

From the Heart

In 2011 Beyoncé released her fourth album, *4*. Talking of the album in her 2013 documentary, *Life Is But a Dream*, she said: "I'm going to forget being cool. I'm going to be honest, I'm going to be sad, I'm going to be passionate, I'm going to be vulnerable, I'm going to sing from my heart."

Before 2016's *Lemonade*, *4* featured Beyoncé's most personal, vulnerable and powerful collection of songs, spawning a staggering seven singles – 'Run the World (Girls)', 'Best Thing I Never Had', 'Party', 'Love On Top', 'Countdown', 'I Care' and 'End of Time' – and sold more than 5 million copies worldwide.

4 is the Magic Number

Beyoncé's lucky number is four.

She was born on 4 September. Jay-Z was born on 4 December. Her mother, Tina, was born on 4 January. She married Jay-Z on 4 April (the fourth day of the fourth month). Her fourth studio album is called *4* and Jay-Z's 2017 album was called *4.44*.

To celebrate the number's significance even further, the Roman numeral for four (IV) is tattooed on Beyoncé and Jay-Z's ring fingers.

Baby Blue

Beyoncé's first pregnancy announcement was pretty unusual. She made the declaration live, onstage, while performing 'Love On Top' to an audience of 12.5 million people during the 2011 MTV Video Music Awards!

"I want you to feel the love that's growing inside of me," she proclaimed before unbuttoning her sequined blazer and rubbing her baby bump.

This iconic moment broke the Guinness World Record for most Tweets posted per second during a single event: 8,868!

Surprise!

Not for the first or last time, Beyoncé revolutionized the music industry when, in December 2013, she released her fifth studio album, *Beyoncé*, on Apple's iTunes without any promotion or messaging. This "surprise album" release strategy has now become the new normal for many of the world's biggest artists.

Beyoncé chose this method after her previous album, *4*, was leaked a month before release. As a result, *Beyoncé* became the fastest-selling album in the history of iTunes within three days of its release.

> "It was important to me that I gave myself time to focus on becoming the woman I want to be, building my empire, my relationship, and my self-worth, before I became a mother."

Beyoncé, *The Hollywood Reporter*, October 2011

The Most Famous Baby
in the World

In January 2012, Beyoncé and Jay-Z's daughter Blue Ivy Carter was born.

On the day, *Time* magazine called the infant "the most famous baby in the world". Indeed, Blue Ivy became the youngest human to be heard on a charted song – a Guinness World Record, FYI – as proud daddy Jay-Z recorded her cute coos, cries and heartbeats and featured them on his song 'Glory', released two days after she was born.

Extra Jalapeños, Please

Beyoncé's favourite indulgence? Pizza. Her topping of choice? Extra tomato sauce with jalapeños. Now you know!

Beyoncé has been visiting her favourite pizza spot, Lucali, in Carroll Gardens, Brooklyn, New York, for more than a decade. If you go, the pepperoni chips are a must.

"If you see me on TV, I'm not a humble, shy person, but it's a transformation into that. It's a job. In real life I'm not like that."

Beyoncé, *Rolling Stone*, March 2004

The Mrs Carter Show

Beyoncé's fifth world tour, 2013–14's Mrs Carter Show is the artist's longest tour to date and her first as a new mother. Check it out:

- ★ More than 130 shows in total across five continents.

- ★ 22 songs performed to more than 2 million fans.

- ★ Grossed $229 million (£170 million) – at the time making it one of the world's most profitable tours ever for a female artist.

- ★ Packed with elaborate sets, costume changes, dynamic choreography and pyrotechnics.

- ★ Toddler Blue Ivy joined her mother on stage once or twice to say hello to fans!

Making a Super Statement

At the 2016 Super Bowl halftime show, Beyoncé appeared as a guest of British rockers Coldplay. She performed her new song 'Formation' – released the day before – and it instantly became a political and cultural statement too important to ignore.

It became Google's most-searched song in 2016 due in part to its controversial music video, with its anti-police themes and message. The video also received critical acclaim, with *Rolling Stone* naming it the greatest music video of all time in 2021.

"Glastonbury really is the biggest festival in the world and I cannot wait to perform there. I'm pumped just thinking about that huge audience and soaking up their energy."

Beyoncé, *Billboard*, February 2011

Making Glasto History

On 26 June 2011, Beyoncé became the first black artist to headline the UK's largest festival – Glastonbury. It was a triumphant, career-defining, universally acclaimed 25-song set that drew the biggest crowd in the 40-year history of the festival – more than 175,000!

Over 2.6 million viewers watched her performance broadcast on the BBC, a figure that at the time broke the record for most television views for a single performance.

The success of Beyoncé's set ushered in a decade-long demand for solo female pop headliners, including Adele (2016), Katy Perry (2017), Billie Eilish (2022), Miley Cyrus (2019), Taylor Swift (2020, cancelled due to COVID-19) and Dua Lipa (2024).

Beyoncé

THAT Baby Bump Photo

In 2017, Queen Bey broke the internet. Again.
The artist released a photo: Beyoncé sitting on
her knees in front of a floral arch, a veil over her
head, with her hands placed on her pregnant
belly, announcing the imminent arrival of twins,
Rumi and Sir.

Within days, the iconic image had more than
11 million likes. It became Instagram's most-
liked post that year and sent her 300 million
followers into a frenzy.

"We would like to share our love and happiness. We have been blessed two times over."

Beyoncé, *Instagram*, February 2017

Essential Album #5: *Cowboy Carter*

On 29 March 2024, Beyoncé released her eighth studio album, *Cowboy Carter*, the second album (after *Renaissance*) to be credited with Beyoncé as primary songwriter for all 27 tracks (bar 'Jolene').

The record is considered a masterpiece: Beyoncé's reinvention of Americana shone a spotlight on lesser-known Black country artists such as Tanner Adell, Brittney Spencer, Tiera Kennedy, Reyna Roberts, Shaboozey and Willie Jones, and was both brave and controversial.* Unfortunately, the album was snubbed by the Country Music Awards (CMAs).

*The album also features collaborations with other country artists, including Miley Cyrus, Dolly Parton, Post Malone and Willie Nelson.

\\ "At this point, I really know who I am, and don't feel like I have to put myself in a box. I'm not afraid of taking risks – no one can define me. \\

Beyoncé, EW.com, May 2011

" I am still a bit in shock that I'm a part of this film because I grew up watching *The Lion King*. It's the first Disney movie that brought me to tears. "

Beyoncé, on ABC's *Good Morning America*, July 2019

Happy B-day

More Than a Disney Princess

In 2019, Beyoncé voiced the character of Nala for Disney's live action version of the beloved animated film, *The Lion King*. It was a blockbuster, earning more than $1.5 billion (£1 billion). She also lent her vocals to two classic songs, 'Can You Feel the Love Tonight' and 'Spirit'.

The film was so successful that it inspired Beyoncé to direct the visual album *Black Is King* (2020) for Disney+, a project that used songs from the film to celebrate Black heritage, featuring important African artists.

Beyoncé

A Cool One-bill

Beyoncé's 'Single Ladies (Put a Ring on It)'
is teetering on hitting a historic milestone on
YouTube: more than 1 billion views.

Released in 2008, the song quickly became an
anthem due in part to the now-iconic black-and-
white minimalist video and, without doubt, one of
the most imitated dance routines in music history.

Beyoncé wanted the famous choreography
(based on a dance style known as "J-Setting")
to appear as if filmed in one take, but the three
dancers actually performed it 50 times on the day.

Practice Makes Perfect

For her complex dance routine in the 'Single Ladies (Put a Ring on It)' music video, self-proclaimed perfectionist Beyoncé practiced the choreography *every day for six weeks* to ensure that come the time of the shoot, her performance was seamless.

During filming, Beyoncé broke three pairs of high heels. If you look closely, you can see the change from one pair of heels to a new pair.

One of the All-time Greats

In 2023, *Rolling Stone* produced their definitive list of the 200 greatest singers of all time. As you'd expect, the Top 10 is pretty extraordinary – and Beyoncé and Mariah Carey are the only two modern-era singers to make it.

1. Aretha Franklin (Beyoncé would agree!)
2. Whitney Houston
3. Sam Cooke
4. Billie Holiday
5. Mariah Carey
6. Ray Charles
7. Stevie Wonder
8. Beyoncé
9. Otis Redding
10. Al Green

Happy B-day

Black Parade

On Juneteenth (19 June) 2020, the day when the USA celebrates the abolishment of slavery and black culture, Beyoncé released the single 'Black Parade'. The song was a call to arms to halt police brutality in the wake of the murder of George Floyd, which had taken place a month earlier. All proceeds from the single were donated to Black-owned businesses.

The track debuted at No. 1 on the Billboard Digital Song Sales chart and won Best R'n'B Performance at the 2021 Grammys.

Chapter Four

Run the World

"I'm over being
a pop star.
I don't want
to be a hot girl.
I want to be
iconic."

Beyoncé, *Marie Claire*, October 2008

Beyoncé is one of the biggest artists of all time, selling more than 174 million solo albums across eight studio albums, according to the Recording Institute of American Artists (RIAA).

Of course, that's only half the story. Beyoncé has sold an additional 60 million records as one-third of Destiny's Child, across five studio albums.

Cover Woman

When Beyoncé appeared on the September 2018 issue of *Vogue* – the world's most iconic fashion magazine – it was a huge moment for Black culture.

Not only was Bey the first African-American woman in the magazine's history to take creative control of a cover shoot, it was also the first time a Black photographer – 23-year-old Tyler Mitchell – shot the cover, at the request of the singer.

"When I first started, 21 years ago, I was told that it was hard for me to get onto covers of magazines because Black people did not sell. Clearly that has been proven a myth."

Beyoncé, *Vogue*, September 2018

'Run the World' is definitely riskier than something a bit more simple. I can never be safe; I always try and go against the grain. As soon as I accomplish one thing, I just set a higher goal. That's how I've gotten to where I am.

Beyoncé, *Billboard*, May 2011

Going Against the Grain

Fierce, sassy, powerful, intense, aggressive, relentless – all of these words describe perfectly Beyoncé's 2011 electropop tune 'Run the World (Girls)', a live fan favourite thanks to its extreme choreography, stunning visuals and celebration of female empowerment. The song wasn't a huge hit, but it represented a feminist message that Beyoncé wanted to be part of.

The Beyoncé Effect

The Beyoncé effect is a term used by cultural commentators and the Beyhive to describe Beyoncé's influence over trends once brands feature her creative artistry. Put simply: anything Beyoncé touches turns to gold.

A famous example is when Beyoncé and Jay-Z filmed their 2018 'Apeshit' music video at the Louvre, Paris. The museum's annual visitor count increased by 25 per cent (to 10.2 million) in the year after the video's release.

"The world will see you the way you see you and treat you the way you treat yourself."

Beyoncé, *New Republic*, 27 January 2013

Be Good Now

Founded in 2013, Beyoncé's BeyGOOD Foundation is a non-profit global charitable initiative focused on providing aid, food and funds to help disaster relief, small businesses and public health.

The foundation raised more than $6 million (£5 million) during the COVID-19 pandemic, and more than $12 million (£10 million) to support victims in the aftermath of Houston's Hurricane Harvey in 2017.

Elevating Athleisure

Beyoncé is more than just a style icon
– she's a style empire!

In 2016, she created Ivy Park, a brand of athletic
leisure (or "athleisure") that gives fans a chance
to wear Beyoncé's unique sports fashion style.

Today, each new collection sells out
within 24 hours, and the brand is valued at
more than $400 million (£335 million).

Presidential Approval

Hailed by the singer as "the biggest moments of my life" (*Harper's Bazaar*, 2011) Beyoncé's performances at both of President Barack Obama's inauguration events are now historic.

For the first inauguration ball, in January 2009, Beyoncé sang Etta James's 'At Last' during the first dance between the President and First Lady Michelle Obama.

In January 2013, the singer took to the Capitol stage for the second inauguration to belt out the 'Star Spangled Banner' as 1 million Americans gathered in Washington D.C. and a further 22 million watched at home.

Michelle Obama told me she was very happy that her girls have someone like me to look up to... And I'm like, 'Oh, my God'.

Beyoncé, *Vogue*, April 2009

Behind the Camera

Of course, Beyoncé is far more than a singer-songwriter and performer. Since 2008, she's also been a filmmaker, directing eight full-length movies, including five concert films and two musical films – with a combined gross income of more than $2.5 billion (£2 billion)!

1. *I Am... World Tour* (2010)
2. *Live at Roseland: Elements of 4* (2011)
3. *Life Is But a Dream* (2013)
4. *Live in Atlantic City* (2013)
5. *Lemonade: A Visual Album* (2016)
6. *Homecoming: A Film by Beyoncé* (2019)
7. *Black Is King* (2020)
8. *Renaissance: A Film by Beyoncé* (2023)

Oscar-worthy

2022 was the year that Beyoncé received an
Oscar nomination for Best Original Song,
'Be Alive', which featured in *King Richard* (2021),
the sports biopic based on Venus and
Serena Williams' father.

"During my recovery from the birth of my twins, I gave myself self-love and self-care, and I embraced being curvier. I accepted what my body wanted to be. After six months, I started preparing for Coachella. But I was patient with myself and enjoyed my fuller curves. My kids and husband did, too."

Beyoncé, *Vogue*, August 2018

Coachella Queens

Beyoncé's headline set at Coachella Festival, California, in 2018 is considered one of the most iconic in the festival's history – and for good reason.

1. It became the most-watched live Coachella performance on YouTube during the livestream.

2. It saw the singer reunite with Kelly Rowland and Michelle Williams for the first time since 2006.

3. It was the first time a Black female artist headlined the festival.

Just 10 of Bey's World Records

1. Most wins at the MTV Video Music Awards

2. Most Grammy awards won by a female artist

3. Most Grammy awards won by a married couple

4. First female artist to win best Rap Performance at the Grammys

5. Most current Twitter engagements (average retweets) for a female musician

6. First act to debut at No. 1 with their first six studio albums (USA)

7. Highest earning couple in Hollywood ever

8. Highest annual earnings for a female singer

9. Most Grammy nominations in a single year for a female artist

10. Most Grammy nominations for a female artist

Beyoncé is the biggest star in the Guinness World Records Hall of Fame, the pantheon of the world's greatest record-breakers. Right now, she holds 20 world records, more than any other female pop singer.

The Renaissance Period

After *Lemonade*, Beyoncé returned in 2022 with her seventh studio album, *Renaissance*, her most powerful record to date. It celebrated themes of Black LGBTQ+ culture to the sounds of house and disco, and was the first album of a new trilogy, with *Cowboy Carter* (2024) the second instalment.

Renaissance was a huge success with her fans. As was its accompanying world tour, grossing more than $550 million (£410 million), across 56 shows.

The Renaissance World Tour currently stands as the seventh highest-grossing concert tour of all time, and the highest-grossing tour by a female artist, second only to Taylor Swift's Eras Tour.

〝I wanted everyone to take a minute to research on the word cowboy. Up to a quarter of all cowboys were Black. These men faced a world that refused to see them as equal, and yet the cowboy is a symbol of strength and aspiration in America.〞

Beyoncé, GQ, September 2024

Cowgirl Carter

With the release of *Cowboy Carter*, her eighth studio album, in March 2024, Beyoncé became the *first Black female artist* to top Billboard's Hot Country Songs chart in the modern history of America's country music. Wow.

La Casa de Castille

In May 2023, Beyoncé and Jay-Z purchased the most expensive house ever sold in Malibu, California.

The estate complex is a 15,000 square-foot (1,400 square-metre), 11-bedroom mansion. They call it La Casa de Castille. It cost a reported $200 million (£150 million). Worth every penny, no doubt.

❯❯People see celebrities, and they have money and fame. But I'm a human being. I get scared and I get nervous just like everyone else.❮❮

Beyoncé, *The Hollywood Reporter*, January 2013

"You can't let anyone tell you what your best is. You know what your best is."

Beyoncé, *The Piers Morgan Show*, 2011

She Can Pay Her Own Bills, Bills, Bills

Today, Beyoncé's net worth is estimated by *Forbes* to be valued at more than $760 million (£565 million), making her one of America's wealthiest self-made women.

Most of Beyoncé's wealth comes from her music, tours, films, Ivy Park fashion and brand/product endorsements, which have included L'Oréal, Tommy Hilfiger, Giorgio Armani, Pepsi, H&M and Adidas.

Rolling Stone's Essential Songs

To celebrate Beyoncé's meteoric rise to the pantheon of performers, *Rolling Stone* made a list of her Top 10 most essential – and most important – songs.

1. 'Déjà Vu,' ft. Jay-Z (2006)
2. 'Formation' (2016)
3. 'Crazy In Love' (2003)
4. 'Sorry' (Homecoming Live) (2019)
5. 'Love On Top' (2011)
6. 'Me, Myself and I' (2003)
7. 'Partition' (2013)
8. 'Love Drought' (2016)
9. 'Single Ladies (Put a Ring on It)' (2008)
10. 'Dangerously In Love 2' (2003)

"She's incredibly talented. She's what every female artist should strive to be like. Despite all her success, she still remains humble."

Rihanna, *Jingle Ball*, 2005

"Beyoncé is the most important and compelling popular musician of the 21st century. It's not just that she's a dazzling, gale-force performer. She's got the finest set of ears, the sharpest musical mind, of anyone in her pop generation."

Jody Rosen, *The New Yorker*, 20 February 2013